Exploring World Cultures
Ireland

Ann Poeschel

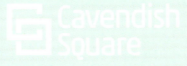

Published in 2018 by Cavendish Square Publishing, LLC
243 5th Avenue, Suite 136, New York, NY 10016

Copyright © 2018 by Cavendish Square Publishing, LLC

First Edition

No part of this publication may be reproduced, stored in a retrieval system, or transmitted in any form or by any means—electronic, mechanical, photocopying, recording, or otherwise—without the prior permission of the copyright owner. Request for permission should be addressed to Permissions, Cavendish Square Publishing, 243 5th Avenue, Suite 136, New York, NY 10016. Tel (877) 980-4450; fax (877) 980-4454.

Website: cavendishsq.com

This publication represents the opinions and views of the author based on his or her personal experience, knowledge, and research. The information in this book serves as a general guide only. The author and publisher have used their best efforts in preparing this book and disclaim liability rising directly or indirectly from the use and application of this book.

All websites were available and accurate when this book was sent to press.

Library of Congress Cataloging-in-Publication Data

Names: Poeschel, Ann, author.
Title: Ireland / Ann Poeschel.
Description: New York : Cavendish Square Publishing, [2018] |
Series: Exploring world cultures | Includes index.
Identifiers: LCCN 2017016348 (print) | LCCN 2017016505 (ebook) | ISBN 9781502630155 (pbk.) |
ISBN 9781502630179 (library bound) | ISBN 9781502630162 (6 pack) | ISBN 9781502630186 (E-book)
Subjects: LCSH: Ireland--Juvenile literature.
Classification: LCC DA906 (ebook) | LCC DA906 .P63 2018 (print) |
DDC 941.7--dc23
LC record available at https://lccn.loc.gov/2017016348

Editorial Director: David McNamara
Editor: Kristen Susienka
Copy Editor: Alex Tessman
Associate Art Director: Amy Greenan
Designer: Graham Abbott
Production Coordinator: Karol Szymczuk
Photo Research: J8 Media

The photographs in this book are used by permission and through the courtesy of: Cover Blaine Harrington III/Alamy Stock Photo; p. 5 Richard Semik/Shutterstock.com; p. 6 Pavalena/Shutterstock.com; p. 7 Patryk Kosmider/Shutterstock.com; p. 8 Mikroman6/Moment/Getty Images; p. 9 DEA/G. Dagli Orti/Getty Images; p. 10 Stefano Zaccaria/Shutterstock.com; p. 11 Orlando Sierra/AFP/Getty Images; p. 12 SidBradypus/Shutterstock.com; p. 13 Semmick Photo/Shutterstock.com; p. 14 Bernard Golden/Alamy Stock Photo; p. 15 Sean Hopson/Alamy Stock Photo; p. 16 Joe FoxBerlin/Radharc Images/Alamy Stock Photo; p. 17 Peter Unger/Lonely Planet Images/Getty Images; p. 18 Rieger Bertrand/Hemis/Alamy Stock Photo; 19 Peter Zoeller/Design Pics/Getty Images; p. 20 Stephen Long/Shutterstock.com; p. 21 Historical Picture Archive/Corbis/Getty Images; p. 22 Robert Alexander/Getty Images; p. 23 Phil Crean A./Alamy Stock Photo; p. 24 Brian Lawless/PA Images/Alamy Stock Photo; p. 26 Piaras Ó Mídheach/Sportsfile/Getty Images; p. 28 Karl Allgaeuer/Shutterstock.com.

Printed in the United States of America

Contents

Introduction		4
Chapter 1	Geography	6
Chapter 2	History	8
Chapter 3	Government	10
Chapter 4	The Economy	12
Chapter 5	The Environment	14
Chapter 6	The People Today	16
Chapter 7	Lifestyle	18
Chapter 8	Religion	20
Chapter 9	Language	22
Chapter 10	Arts and Festivals	24
Chapter 11	Fun and Play	26
Chapter 12	Food	28
Glossary		30
Find Out More		31
Index and About the Author		32

Introduction

Ireland is a country in the **European Union**. People have lived in Ireland for a long time. Rocks, buildings, and artwork of ancient civilizations can still be found here. In the past, Ireland faced difficult times, but today the Republic of Ireland is an independent country.

Famous symbols of Ireland are the harp, the shamrock, and the Celtic cross. Music, dancing, art, and literature are important parts of Irish culture. People enjoy playing and watching sports. The Irish people are friendly and like to have fun. They hold many festivals throughout the year. At the end of a long day, they like to spend time with family and friends.

Ireland has beautiful scenery. You can do many outdoor activities there. Many people like to take walks, ride their bikes, and explore nature. Ireland has amazing beaches and coastlines. It is a beautiful country to live in and explore.

Bantry Bay is a beautiful coastline in West Cork.

Geography

Ireland is an island. The Atlantic Ocean surrounds it. The Irish Sea separates it from Great Britain. The island is divided into two parts: the Republic of Ireland and Northern Ireland. Northern Ireland is part of the United Kingdom.

This map shows the two parts of Ireland.

Much of Ireland's land is for farming. In fact, 61 percent is farmland, and 10 percent is forestland.

People sometimes call Ireland "the Emerald Isle." That is because it is so green there. It has grassy plains, mountains, and coastlines. It also has many lakes and rivers. The longest river is called the River Shannon.

Ireland gets a lot of rain. This keeps the grass and trees green. Temperatures vary from 30 degrees Fahrenheit (–1 degree Celsius) in winter to 70 degrees Fahrenheit (21°C) in summer.

Famous Cliffs

The Cliffs of Moher are famous in Ireland. They were formed over three hundred million years ago!

The Cliffs of Moher

History

Humans first lived in Ireland in 6000 BCE. Ancient people called Gaels lived there after. Other groups ruled there later, too. In 433 CE, Saint Patrick arrived in Ireland and converted people to Christianity. Ireland became part of the United Kingdom in 1801.

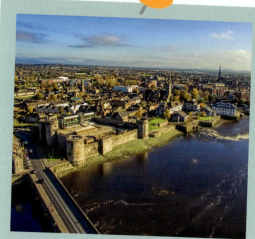

Today, Ireland's cities are a mix of old and new buildings.

Not everyone liked that, though. **Uprisings** took place. In 1916, a man named Padráig (PADRIG) Pearse declared Ireland's independence. This day was called the Easter Rising. It started a civil war, which ended in 1921. Then Ireland became divided. Six counties in the north

Ancient groups in Ireland built large tombs that still exist today.

remained with the United Kingdom. The rest formed the new Irish Free State.

Ireland's **constitution** was formed in 1937. In 1949, the Republic of Ireland became completely independent. Today, the Republic of Ireland is a **democracy**.

Newgrange is an ancient tomb surrounded by carved stones.

Potato Famine

The Great Potato Famine happened in Ireland in the 1840s. Many people died or moved away to escape it.

Government

Dublin is the capital city of the Republic of Ireland. It is home to the National Parliament, called the Oireachtas (irr-OCK-tuss). The National Parliament consists of the president and two houses of parliament.

The president is the head of state and the armed forces. He or she oversees the work of the two houses of parliament.

Leinster House in Dublin is home to the Irish Parliament.

Mary Robinson became Ireland's first female president in 1990.

The houses of parliament are called Dáil Éireann (DAWL erin) and Seanad Éireann (SHAN-ED erin). Dáil Éireann is led by the prime minister, called the *taoiseach* (TEE-shock). The taoiseach leads the government.

Courts help make sure laws are followed in Ireland. There is a supreme court that handles tough problems.

Mary Robinson

Ireland's Flag

The Irish flag is green, orange, and white. It is a symbol of unity among the Irish people. Green is for **Irish republicans**, orange for Protestants, and white for peace between them.

11

The Economy

The Republic of Ireland is a popular place for businesses. Dublin and Cork are important cities for technology. Companies such as Apple, Facebook, and Google have their European headquarters in Ireland.

The Samuel Beckett Bridge in Dublin moves so ships can access the river.

As a member of the European Union, the Republic of Ireland's currency is the euro.

Ireland's **economy** used to rely on farming and making machines. The country's economy grew in the 1990s and 2000s. This time was called the Celtic

Ryanair

In 2015, Irish-based Ryanair became the first airline to carry more than one hundred million international passengers in a single year.

Passengers board a Ryanair plane.

Tiger. Today, Ireland has many different industries. Technology, medicine, food, and tourism help make Ireland successful.

Ireland also sends products to other countries to keep its economy healthy. They sell medicines, computers, and food all over the world.

The Environment

Ireland has a lot of natural beauty and it's important to protect it. Irish people value a clean and healthy environment. They have some of the best air, water, and soil in Europe. However, there are some troubles.

Power

Many Irish people use different kinds of energy to get electricity. Waterpower and wind power are the two largest alternative energy sources.

The Republic of Ireland has over two hundred wind farms.

Fungie the friendly dolphin lives in Dingle Bay, County Kerry.

In Ireland, pollution is a concern. Many people travel by car. Cars produce **emissions**, which can damage the environment.

The country tries to take care of the environment.

Almost 20 percent of Ireland's land is covered in peat.

One way they do this is by encouraging people to ride their bikes. In Dublin, almost eleven thousand people ride bikes to work every day.

Many animals and plants live in Ireland. **Peat** is common There is also a large dolphin, whale, and seal population.

15

The People Today

Ireland is a small country. There are over 4.9 million people living there.

Many people living in Ireland have proud Irish roots and good jobs. Some work in business, others in hotels or restaurants, and others as teachers, tour guides, doctors, and police officers. Most families live in houses or apartments.

People enjoy a sunny day in a Dublin park.

Travelers

A community called the Irish Travelers is a minority in Ireland. They have their own unique heritage and identity.

Today, many immigrants are arriving in the country. They bring new traditions and customs to the country and help make Ireland a more exciting place.

FACT!

Ireland's largest city is Dublin. Over 1.2 million people live there.

Many people in other countries have Irish ancestors. In the 1800s and 1900s, some Irish families traveled to the United States, Canada, and other parts of the world to live. Many people are proud of their Irish heritage.

Brightly colored houses in Dublin stand before the River Liffey.

Lifestyle

Irish people are very welcoming and are known for their sense of humor. They love to have fun and good times. They value community and family.

Many families are large and have a strong bond. Some families have five or more children.

A classroom in Ireland

Children start school young. When older, many children will go on to a university or college.

In Ireland, a person can vote when they turn eighteen years old.

About 63 percent of people living in Ireland live in cities. Big cities include Dublin, Cork, and Limerick. People in Ireland travel on buses, trains, and in cars to get around the country. They use ferries to travel to the islands and to Great Britain.

Many people use buses to travel in Ireland's big cities.

Women have an important role in society. They have important jobs and are members of political parties.

O the Irish

The "O" in Irish names like O'Brien means "descended from." It lets people know someone has Irish heritage.

Religion

Religion is a major part of Irish history and heritage. The Catholic Church especially influenced Irish society after the war of independence. Since then, much violence on the island has been related to religion.

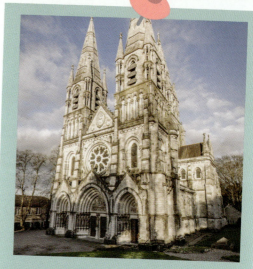
Saint Fin Barre's Cathedral stands in the city of Cork.

Today, Christianity is the main religion of Ireland. Eighty-four percent of people in the Republic of Ireland are Roman Catholic, while 3 percent are Protestant. They worship in churches.

Even though the major religion is Christianity, not all Irish people are Christians. In fact, today,

One of the most beautiful copies of the Gospels in the Bible is in Dublin. It is called the Book of Kells.

many people are choosing to have no religion. In the Republic of Ireland, the largest non-Christian religion is Islam. Muslims make up the third-largest religious group in the country. They worship in mosques.

The Book of Kells is located in Trinity College Dublin.

Saint Patrick's Day

Every year, people of Irish descent all over the world celebrate Saint Patrick's Day on March 17.

Language

Irish and English are the official languages of the Republic of Ireland. Street signs and place names are written in both languages. Laws are also written in both. All students must study Irish in school.

Irish is one of the oldest written languages. An alphabet called the Ogham alphabet was used to write the early Irish language. It is made up of lines often carved into stone. You can find parts of these carvings all across Ireland.

Street signs in Ireland are written in both Irish and English.

Over 38 percent of people living in Ireland speak Irish as a first or second language.

Languages from other countries are also spoken in Ireland. Many immigrants speak their native languages at home and with family. Polish and French are the two most commonly spoken languages after Irish and English.

Ogham stones stand in the Stone Corridor at University College Cork.

Gaeltachts

Gaeltachts (gail-TOCHTS) are regions where the majority of the population speaks Irish. Irish children can visit a Gaeltacht to learn Irish.

23

Arts and Festivals

Ireland has many arts festivals, music festivals, and other outdoor events. St. Patrick's Festival in March is one of the largest celebrations of the year. Everyone gets the day off, and there are parades all over the country.

People celebrate Saint Patrick's Day with large parades across the country.

Ireland is known for its literature. Famous authors include James Joyce, Oscar Wilde, and William Butler Yeats.

Dancing and music are important in Ireland. Traditional Irish dancing is taught in schools.

FACT!

Michael Flatley is a famous Irish dancer who can tap his foot thirty-five times per second. He is in the Guinness Book of World Records.

People dance at gatherings called *céilís* (CAY-lees). Ireland is famous for Riverdance, a popular performance featuring Irish dancers.

Musicians often gather to play traditional music. They use instruments such as the bodhrán (BOH-ran), uilleann (ILL-in) pipes, tin whistle, and fiddle.

Ireland and Halloween

Halloween began in Ireland as the Samhain (sow-in) celebration. It is the country's oldest festival.

Fun and Play

There are many fun things to do in Ireland. Irish people enjoy outdoor activities when the weather is nice. There are lots of coastal walks, beautiful beaches, and parks. Many cities also offer museums and art galleries.

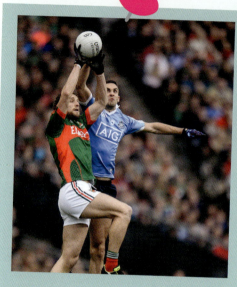

Gaelic football is a popular Irish sport.

Blarney Stone

In Irish folklore, you will be a great speaker if you kiss the stone at Blarney Castle. Every year, tourists go to the castle to kiss the Blarney Stone.

Two brothers from Cork won Ireland's first medal in rowing in the 2016 Olympics.

Irish sport is a popular pastime. The Gaelic Athletic Association (GAA) organizes the national games of Ireland. The major Irish games include hurling, camogie, and Gaelic football. These games have been around for centuries, with ties back to the ancient Celts. They are loved by children and adults.

Many people enjoy other sports too. Other popular sports include soccer, rugby, and rowing.

Food

Traditional Irish meals are simple but hearty. Examples of these meals are Irish stew and colcannon. Meat pie and potatoes is also a common Irish dish.

Tea is an important part of Irish culture. People drink it several times a day. Having a cup of tea is called a "cuppa." It is served at every meal and enjoyed by people of all ages.

Irish stew is a traditional dish made with meat and potatoes.

FACT!

Corned beef and cabbage is not a popular Irish dish, even though many people think it is. Instead, bacon and cabbage is much more popular there.

Ireland has many pubs where people gather to eat and drink and be social. Pubs are local meeting places for sharing good times with friends and family. Many pubs offer meals, snacks, and live music.

Butter!

The city of Cork was once the largest butter market in the world. Today, it is home to the Cork Butter Museum.

Glossary

constitution — A document that lists the country's laws.

democracy — A country that has its leaders elected by the people.

economy — A system of goods or services that helps make a country successful.

emissions — Chemicals or gases given off by a car.

European Union — A group of countries in Europe that make decisions together and usually have the same money.

Irish republicans — People who believe that Ireland should be its own country.

peat — Brown earthy material found in bogs used for fuel.

uprisings — Acts of rebellion.

Find Out More

Books

Burke, Fatti, and John Burke. *Irelandopedia: An Adventure Around Ireland, A Compendium of Maps, Facts and Knowledge.* Dublin, Ireland: Gill and Macmillan, 2015.

Waldron, Melanie. *Ireland.* Countries Around the World. Oxford, UK: Raintree, 2012.

Website

Ask About Ireland

http://askaboutireland.ie

Video

Geography Kids: IRELAND!

https://www.youtube.com/watch?v=OLrWRPBO3iY

Discover the culture, customs, and habits of the Irish people in this video.

Index

constitution, 9

democracy, 9

economy, 12–13

emissions, 15

European Union, 4, 12

immigrants, 17, 23

Irish republicans, 11

peat, 15

uprisings, 8

About the Author

Ann Poeschel earned her bachelor's degree in English from the University of Kansas in 2009. She loves to travel and experience new cultures. A native of Kansas, she now lives in Edinburgh, Scotland, in the United Kingdom.